Desolation and Epiphany

By

James W. A.

To my sister Elizabeth,

though I believe your prayers made it possible,
I wish you could see the man I've become
and hope you will someday.

Desolation:
"Darkness of soul, disturbance in it, movement to things low and earthly, the unquiet of different agitations and temptations, moving to want of confidence, without hope, without love, when one finds oneself all lazy, tepid, said, and as if separated from his Creator and Lord." - St. Ignatius of Loyola

Epiphany:
"Longing for God has its roots in the past, yet does not remain there: It reaches out to the future... We need to set out anew each day, in life as in faith, for faith is not a suit of armor that encases us; instead, it is a fascinating journey, a constant and restless movement, ever in search of God, always discerning our way forward." - Pope Francis

Contents

Princes of a Soul's State

Welcome to a wondrous display of
beauty, vanity, humor, and sorrow,
a tragedy of squander and a comedy of enlightenment.

There will be two players on this stage,
two voices you will hear as your witness
the dreams they've had and will forever
in the pages of this book.

I will introduce you to them now:

The first we will call "Desolation."
He is naive and arrogant,
like you yourself may have once been or,
Heaven forbid, still are.

He will share with you cries and musings
that were born from a heart that suffers
under the weight of its brokenness and nihilism;
His dreams are dark and not to be trusted,
but they are not always to be dismissed either.
Take care if you find yourself believing in his flaws,
for it may be a sign for you, reader,
to examine your own heart and life.

The second, we have named "Epiphany."
He is young and wise,
for he has been reborn from a past's Hell
by a miracle of grace.

He will share with you stories and observations
that were gleaned from a mind redeemed,
that sees and creates joys in all things;
His dreams are of light and to be savored,
but they are not absolute, nor infallible.
It is good to revel in his elation, but
let it grow and expand, dear reader,
lest you stagnate your own mind and life.

Remember the speakers in this collection,
their perspectives, impartings, and stances.
They stand strong in the shadows and spotlight,
needed for each other for the journey to be complete,
both as they are a part of many's journeys,
and to understand the shades of each in the other,
as neither are damned, nor perfect.

Please enjoy and reflect on these words
knowing that I am grateful for your company.

Without further ado, let us raise the curtain
and witness a soul laid bare:
The spectacle of Desolation and Epiphany.

I

Desolation

Me

why am I lying here
brooding, gasping, crying
pathetically

we all have black nights
I don't really want to kill

Do I?

I have this fantasy, you know
not a sexual one, just a dream
where you and I take nothing
and run, we ride, to everywhere

I have my book
you have your beauty
and that's all
not money, not blood
not any wayward obligations

just lust, we drive

but you couldn't understand
how could you
after all, you can't see it

after all, you're not
like me

Are you?

The Right Time to Lie

I've always asserted
that I've "had my reasons"
for the wretched things I do,
but the truth is
that indecision,
that cowardice,
is just as much to blame.

I've been labeled
(a liar, a traitor, selfish)
by the people
that I like to think
I feel love for.

Deep down, these are
all things that I admire,
but a legacy I don't deserve
when freedom is all
that I truly desire.

I crave peace
despite the truth
that I can't stand for
or, more importantly,
define it.

I hate myself
for being broken
enough to still hurt
7

myself and others
and still remain unchanged.

I live in chaos
because it's familiar
(it's all I know),
always understanding,
yet helpless.

No crown can control me,
nor stability anchor me,
which leaves me here,
in the unenviable position
of sacrificing what I must
for nothing really at all.

Wandering in Sight of the Alleyway

Elusive morning star,
against the twilight sky:
Would you tell me where you are
or would you pass me by?
The clouds and earth are spiral bound,
it seems I've lost my stay,
with dreams by never a compass found,
and bright eyes in the alleyway.

Trees are lining the lonely road,
as they flutter with me in the gust,
leaving me no place to find abode,
yet I still do, as though I must.
Until time comes for me to depart,
for then I will resume my claims:
Let flow in sequence mind and heart,
and repeat their familiar names.

I pass kin smiling, walking along,
their happiness, how could I find?
Struggles are many when made to be wrong,
for one beaten, darkened, and blind.
Every warm-lit home mocks my state,
as this security I cannot possess,
though humbled by voids and their weight
I somehow yearn for any's caress.

But still I press ever onward,
through concrete, sand, or ice,

lest the madness drive me wayward,
humanity is my only vice.
So I sleep with your ghost on moonlit nights
in ways sometimes not the best.
Survival is not one of eternal fights,
perhaps in the alleyway, I'll find my rest.

Denial

Help isn't very helpful to
me when
I'm fixated on what keeps me
alive, and tethered, not
drowning in what I could be
and all that I am. We are never
broken. We are sustained by dreams.

Ill-usion

I woke up enlightened
and, for the haziest of moments,
saw this world as clearly as
all of those that could have been
until the infection of reality
blinded me once more,
until I saw nothing
beyond what was put before me,
tailored by a world uncaring,
save for what could be instilled.

How I long for such a dream again,
to see such a face forevermore.

Rainy-Car Day

Although it wasn't, truly,
a revolutionary notion,
I understand now,
though I should have then,
what you said to me
on that rainy-car day.

I couldn't stomach the irony,
both its dryness and its poison,
and the world spun around,
as it tended to the nights,
I could think of little else,
nor make sense of the sweet cruelty.

What was it you said,
softly, yet distantly,
that impacted me that day,
and wrung a fragile mind
into a self-destructive shrivel?

Who, the fuck, cares?

They'll Drain You Slowly, Man

Scholars, philosophers, and bullshitters
throughout the centuries
have debated the meaning of one tiny word,
and only a handful of visionaries,
        like Tina Turner,
have dared to question its relevancy.

That word is love,
                and opinions on it are as varied
                        as the assholes who deal with it.

The young call it passion,
the poets call it inspiration,
the theologians call it God,
the incels call it sex,
the corporate executives call it revenue,
and some don't believe in it at all.

Do you want to know what I think
                        on such a grandiose subject?

I think that love is simply pain.
I think that it's designed to hurt, thoroughly,
                as you give up all of yourself for another.

Love is spitting blood into a bathroom sink
because you can't stomach her pain.
Love is choking on your own pride

while you smile foolishly, achingly at his antics.
Love is wanting to disgorge all your organs
as you repress your dreams, lose friends, and cast aside family,
but you do it all anyways because
                                        That's. What. Lovers. Do.
Besides, it's the "right thing" to do anyways.

To me, love is both disease and cure,
                            poison and antidote,
                                creation and annihilation.
It is the only thing that your soul is meant for, longs for,
and it is the only thing that can destroy you so completely
that this very thing you were born for
makes you wish that you never had been.

The way I see, the opposite of love isn't hate;
it isn't even apathy, as a kind teacher once told me.
Love is survival, clear and simply put:
Survival against loneliness,
            against damnation,
                against all of the fucked up things we fear,
even though it's more horrifying than all of those combined.

It's because of this, that in my last moments,
with whomever at my side,
I will smile, coldly spinning one final lie,
knowing the belief that I lived to die
has been the opposite truth all along.

This will set me free,
and I wish the same for all of you.
15

Legendary Gose

A shifty man in this, a shifty bar,
watches shifty glances
dance all around him.

It is a gose that he sips,
Should anyone ask;
he cares less than you,   either way,
a primary outlook on life.

At least it was when he had it, life:
A heart that did more than pump blood,
soul worth more than the   highest bidder,
and eyes that did not see truth.

Yes, that pitiful poison, truth:
The scope that reminds him he isn't
legendary as he believes   himself to be
or anything more than the demons' toy.

So he'll keep on playing the toy;
A gear in society's horror,
salty, sour, and   haze-filled,
not unlike this brew that he sips from

as spirits dance around him,
flashing broken glances,
fixated in a broken bar: just a broken man.

Will to Live

It is the moments my mind is lost
within whatever consumes me
that I see *her* smile intoxicatingly
and I know my days are numbered,
though by how many is always debatable.

After all, I've flirted with Death,
        in the ethereal game of chicken
that we engage in most evenings,
more times than are appropriate
for someone in my standing.

What standing might that be?

It is amongst so many voices,
        above, within, below, around,
all laughing as I tumble to a terrifying truth:

Love is life's greatest lie
when it is designed by devils,
        those who seek only dominion,
rather than born by the Heavens
or the Earth, when it cares enough
to grace a life defiled by Hell,
and granted a blessing incorporeal.

It is *this* that I crave above all others,
no matter what my actions may indicate.

Defiant Pursuit

What is it that I lack
that allows wholeness
to be as elusive to me
as the sleep I am also denied?

Is it something inherent,
gifted by a God that
cares more for the chosen
than a forsaken like me,
or were the parts of me
I've sacrificed in my pursuit
of a life I never truly wanted
more valuable than anticipated?

Is a heart necessary to follow dreams?
Are the emotions that have been siphoned
from the crater in my chest
what keep me from lasting peace
and are not weakness and temptation
as I have been always led to believe?

Does a mind need to be complete,
unlike the fractured one I possess,
in order to achieve my desires?
I've never believed in sanity over strategy,
but perhaps a perceived strength
is instead my greatest pitfall?

When one's soul is one's own,
not tributed to powers greater,
could then one's dreams be as well?
My mentors, my captors, sold theirs,
trading world destruction for success;
is this a half-truth or worthwhile?

Are memories, all I have left,
indeed a fuel for my future,
or an anchor to a past far gone?
Mine define my being strongly,
but is this the very construct
that will always hold me back?

I lack all of these answers,
yet I question still their relevancy
if indeed the God of favoritism
has decided that some dreams are valid
while others must be eliminated
to make way the path to glory
for those who "deserve" this honor,
letting all other suffer in contempt.

If I am of this latter faction,
the sleep that I scavenge
will instead be the ultimate refuge
for the dreams I choose to embrace!

Patience, Grace, and the Ever-Dismissive Void

Patience is what I cling to
when all else seems aloof:
The bright light of stars
in an otherwise barren sky
burning millions of light years
from where I stand weeping.

Words of grace fall around me,
yet all that I hear landing
is the sound of my inadequacy:
The silence that cowards use
to justify their inaction,
the faulty wisdom of the damned.

Beauty abounds beyond me,
despite all of the best intentions
and the stoic, futile acceptance
of a life lost lonely in the crowd:
The desolate dirge in my head,
possibilities understandably uncaring.

A Spectrum of Sensations

Yellow is a pin prick:
cold needles from the hospital,
spines on a incensed porcupine,
an assailant's stabbing dagger,
Stinging, they flash yellow.

Purple is a flame burn:
an uncontrollably searing stovetop,
ravenous rays on skin,
irrepressible itching,
Scorching, they flash purple.

Green is a sandpaper rub:
coarseness on my skin,
a terrible cardboard scratch,
gritty concrete planks,
Crawling, they flash green.

Red is a soft caress:
small animals from childhood,
a lover's kind embrace,
lilac fabrics that envelop,
Comforting, they flash red.

Blue is an electric shock:
instantaneous stimulation,
pleasure grasping the body,
crackling mechanical sparks,
Snapping, they flash blue.

Orange is a numb void:
the sensation of nothingness,
elegant emptiness surrounding,
stark sweetness of oblivion,
In the end, they all fade to orange.

Synergy

I laugh,
She laughs,
I cry,
She chokes up,
I whimper,
She shouts,
I dance,
She sleeps,
I sigh,
She cries,
She laughs,
I laugh

Always at the same time,
Never together.

Restless

Has the sun even risen
on this day like all others;
the windows blowing through,
bringing a chilled wind to my bed,
as I lie here stark awake?

Is the room ever moving,
as it seems to be at least;
my mind fixates nowhere,
like a waterfall suspended,
a flower shriveling alone?

Is she even in reality
the way she shines to me;
a goddess of perfection,
like a dream cast in the darkness,
thus from where she has bloomed?

Could I rise as alive in spirit
as gardenias to greet the day;
wandering crowded rooms,
would her face be among them,
would it matter without courage?

Is she truly out there somewhere
writhing as restless as I;
does she long for stormy sky embraces,
to be lovers transcending time,

conquering any space between us?
Could I claim the lost desire
to be a knight-hero once more;
could I serve a queen of glory,
cross omnipotent oceans,
and sail on with hand in hand?

Spotlight

The curtain rises
on an effervescent evening
and entering stage left,
I see the brightest rising star.

The crowds cheer without knowing;
they have no regard for brilliance,
seeing only what is before them,
the illumination of this scene:
Lips a sparkling crimson,
Hair an ebony waterfall,
Eyes to make oaks bow
in the shame they now deserve;
These describe only a fraction
of what I've come to appreciate:
The mind behind the motions,
Wit permeating the words.

As the spectacle fades
I, another shameless face
in the sea of a reveling audience,
marvel still in silent wonder.

Should I fade or be silently sighted,
audacity could not shield me from
inadequacy, obscurity, failure,
granted stay, but never sharing.

This world may be a stage,
yet I shall never grace it
beyond the role that I must play:
as unworthy of the spotlight.

We Have a Place in This World

My worst fear used to be dying,
as it is for so many children,
but now I realize that it's dying alone
believing that those I loved, sacrificed for,
are joyful in my absence.

Yet not as I die, but as I live
do I understand that these memories,
overwhelming emotions of what were,
and these dreams, of what could have been,
are the only things that I have left
of the broken and beautiful worlds
I may or may not leave behind.

With them, in death and in life,
I am never, will never, be truly alone.

Spirits' Dream

Another night gone to the past;
the bed as cold and creeping as
the frost left in my veins,
and the ghost of her still sighing.

> Do you think that spirits dream,
> at least in the way we do?
> Can they see our sorrow, our anguish
> or is it all irrelevant to them?

The clock ticks on like a fiendish heart,
metronome swaying, here and away,
falling, then breaking towards an abyss,
the darkness enjoyed by those asleep.

> I wish to believe that spirits dream,
> but what exactly do they witness?
> Is it their own joys or regrets,
> or the emptiness of those left behind?

Later, I see an angel descending;
wings black as an innocent crow,
only a shimmer of light to the mourners gathered:
The promise that her pain has vanished.

> If we could see their spirits' dreams
> in terms mortals could comprehend:
> We'd see longing and loving silence,
> tears as synchronized as our hearts.

Out of the Fray

If every sip of the brew,
that I took with you smiling,
was a moment I could relive,
time would waver to my will
a thousand more times over.

If I had known then
that a dark stout's stoup
would have been my last
with your light around me,
my tears would have salted
yet left it all the more bitter.

Only memories comfort me
when the visage of you cannot
and I, forsaken but enchanted,
fight the emptiness inside
knowing that despite desires,
I would never fight for you again.

Snowy Winter Ale

Lovely, dark and deep,
my bottle stands before me,
chilled and ever-taunting.

     Frost made his choice,
     but did he understand
     the chaos that howls
     beyond the foam?
     Could he see each
     tiny bubble-eye
     glaring up, like too many
     demanding to go miles,
     yet offering malty solace
     in the safety of his stop?
     Were his promises
     so worthy or so few
     or was there a reason
     he wasn't exhausted
     like I am?

Each sip is lovely, dark and deep,
so I'll remain here until I sleep,
alone and afraid until I sleep.

Mistletoe

I never really understood the custom behind mistletoe,
the purpose of it, I mean.

I'm sure that the ancient Greeks or Druids or whomever
meant well when the chose a certain wintery plant to kiss
under,

and I'm sure that many modern couples
leap at the chance to steal a time-alteringly tender moment
under it
amidst the hustle of holiday life;

I'm even sure that poets and songwriters appreciate
having an easy symbol for connection
to wrap around their words like a present's bow.

But I'm also sure that this mischievous mistletoe,
this tiny taunting twig,
means nothing to me, if she's not around
and maybe that's why I simply don't care
what a sprig's spotlight invites,

when my heart is as pale as the gently falling snow.

The Tailor of St. Petersburg

This story begins with a little Boy
learning to sew from his Mother.
"Be careful what you pour into, kid,"
she tells him kindly,
"because the wrong dream will break your heart."

The Tailor was a lovely woman,
best this City's ever had,
taught her Son far too many things;
he should have learned them from his Dad.
The Old Man was the distant sort,
when he left was such a pity,
so she taught her baby all she knew
and how to navigate this City.

When the Boy grew a little,
he made his first real craft:
a tiny wool mask for his innocent face.
He ran up to show his Mother what he'd done,
crying that he did it, he's doing it!
"That's wonderful," she replied to his excitement,
"but remember that every mask has to breathe."

The Tailor was a wiser woman,
strict as she was soft,
put all the pressure on his world
as she raised him from their loft.
The way the Boy had to grow up,
one might call it such a pity,

but she taught him right and she taught him well
how to navigate this City.

The Boy grew older, his tensions flared,
he toiled tougher and learned more;
his heart hardened amongst the cloths.
He knew too well the lonely shop,
thought he did of the world beyond,
and swore he'd cut it all.
He only broke the Tailor's heart that night
when he shouted above the storm,
and she merely stared him back with a stern warn,
"words have more power than you can control,"
as he slammed behind the door.

Oh the arrogance of the Tailor's Son,
how he forgot his youthful law.
She was forced to cast him out of her life
before he left, just like his Pa.
She knew that time would come, 'tis why she tried
to install in him both smooth and gritty
life's beauty, passion, pain, and fear
and how to navigate this City.

Now the Man walks alone at night,
his clothing he repairs each day.
In those hollow moments by the gulf,
he looks out at the waves, swearing he hears
a haunting whisper beckoning him home.
But when he thinks sanely and forsakes his pride,
all he hears is a cold, kind voice,

like the needle in her hand, tell him that,
"reconciliation is not the same as restoration."

This hardy old Tailor and wayward Son,
with holes no skill could sew,
lead separate lives, her having tried her best
to teach him all that he should know.
And when he gazes out at water still,
beneath a moon both cruel and pretty,
he steels his tears for now he knows
how to truly navigate this City.

Closure

Do the oceans have my answer?
I've walked along their shores
for ages, both innocent and tumultuous,
but their waves brought no comfort
or semblance of permanent healing.
so I left to search beyond...

Does the sky have my answer then?
The blackness outside my window
allures as I glide through it.
stars stare parallel with me,
blankly as the humming engine
and relentless as the wind abound...

Do the mountains have my answer?
I've landed within their cradle
to admire their spiking fingers,
as my own reach for more.
The emptiness expanding as continents,
I explore my new surroundings...

Does the city have my answer now?
Blinding light twirling 'round,
like neon dreams illuminating
all but my much too human soul.
The residents spew wayward wisdom,
but never resonate towards closure.

Where shall I find my answer?

Am I to wander this callous country,
incomplete and fallen here
as a torn, haunted specter?

          Or is it beyond these physical planes,
        in the truth that can sense the question?

Muscle Memory

Muscles always remember
what the brain often forgets
and the heart is too cowardly
to ever learn originally.

Eyes remember to glance away
when the brain wants to absorb
as much as it possibly can
and the heart is undecided.

Tongues remember to lie
when the brain can't organize
and the heart, in it's weakness,
longs to tell all truths.

Lungs remember to breathe
when the brain can't decide on
whether they should or not
and the heart declines its vote.

Ears remember to take in whispers
when the brain tries to as well,
those that madden and strengthen,
though the heart can't tell the difference.

Stomachs remember to stabilize
when the brain, conjuring horrors,
causes violent quakes

and the heart stoically agrees.
Muscles always remember pure
that the brain wars in its duality
and the heart, ever unfaithful,
leads us towards ruin.

Static Space

You taught me once that love is life,
never realizing that life is pain.

What *does* that say about love?
The lessons never added up,
as if that mattered,
because Fate never offers,
it only demands.

Through the desolation and isolation
and all kinds of lost elation,
the truth is the only thing that will always lie

and the truth is: I *will* love you
until I breathe my very last,
a time that can't come soon enough;

Because an end to life is an end to love,
and nothing could be more beautiful.

Becoming Who We Were

I used to have a Demon on my shoulder.
She was kind and loving, merciless,
yet the harshest of taskmasters.

It was she that taught me fear;
what it's like to focus only on
the blood you're spitting,
pleading for your life,
as you watch it collapse around you.

I will always treasure those memories,
for they strengthen at a time
when the present abandons
and comfort in the face of the unknown.

I could not understand it then.

I used to have an Angel on my shoulder.
He was cruel and devious, compassionate,
yet the strongest of teachers.

It was he that taught me pain;
what it's like to believe only in
the scars that burn your skin,
emblazoned by what was meant to save you,
as you watch it slip away.

I will always treasure those lessons,
for they center at such a time

when all else is chaotic,
and elevate in the face of fatigue.

I understand it now:
That experiences make us believe we're complete.

The Lure of the Weizenbock

Have you ever noticed,
    if you stare at just the right angle,
        that power lines seem to go on
                as far as the pitiful eye can see?

        Wooden poles can do this

        by doing nothing but existing,

and yet I can't seem to find my way home
        without first stopping by here for a drink.

        See when that damn brew calls my name,

    The lights and sounds join into
           a malicious, alluring refrain

    that I self-destruct to again and again.

           I can justify it numerous ways:
      Stool is comfy after a working week,
     Florida sun is brutal upon my body,
   Craftsmanship has to be appreciated
Or value is too rare to pass up,

but if I burrow deeper down,

past the bottom of the bottle
        to the bottom of my soul,

I'd find the truths left in the foam:

and the truths are that I am
    little more than a maddened man,
sullenly lonely, compulsively weak,

                    when feelings swarm across my mind.

So I and my troubled brethren
will share this toast together:
To a life berated, lit, and stark,
Far beyond the light and the dark.

Hoped Silly

Alone with St. Ambroise,
I sit here again:
my loyal companion,
my lovely tall friend.

Today had its heaven,
lights forming the way;
No chaos can die though,
this madness inside, so
in hell here I stay,
alone with St. Ambroise
at the end of the day.

Liquor Dreams and Forlorn Memories

There are certain visions I receive
in the fleeting, familiar moments
between faltering into bed
and passing out upon it
after too much lonely liquor.

On those unstable nights,
I can see not clearly enough
the sleeping faces and naked bodies
of those that I've left behind,
and those who have done so to me.

Sometimes, I whisper to them
the secrets I held in my heart
but never released out of fear or mercy;
Sometimes instead they convey to me
what I always wish could have been.

These memories of what never were
spin chaotically in these moments
until my poisoned body can sustain no more,
then there is one final moment of peace
where we can all embrace in oblivion.

This is when the dreams begin to
show me fates that aren't,
realities far beyond it,
and the horrifying truth within:

That tomorrow will be exactly the same.

The Food Chain is More of a Cycle

There are many nights,
and some mornings,
where I eat Pringles,
I die,
and I am born again;

Not necessarily in that order.

Life Goes On

I had a 9 AM call on the day of the Apocalypse,
so I woke up and made coffee at 8:10, as usual.
The other man was a little bit late, but I wasn't offended;
it was a fairly mundane meeting, as expected.

When the rain started falling, I thought to myself,
"Well this should cool things down for a bit, that's nice,"
and then I wondered when I should prepare lunch,
more importantly what I should prepare,
either to cook the last of the meat before it spoiled
or the rest of the bread before it turned stale.
It wasn't until the winds picked up, early afternoon,
that I felt like curling up for a nap.

I awoke a little while later with a soaked face and,
staring up at the permanently darkened sky, sighed saying,
"I should probably get that fixed soon,"
before rolling back over deciding, "no, that can wait until
tomorrow."

Bored

Outside,   in the sunlight,
someone is either having sex,
being murdered,
or a baby is,
        for some reason or another,
crying.

I would love to see only one of those happening.

The Search

Anxious
Edgy
Tired
Lonely
Inadequate
Afraid
Cloudy
Stressed, no,
Overwhelmed
Hurting
Impatient
Upset
Uncertain
Just a little horny
And definitely "done"

I stare at the ceiling trying to describe what I'm feeling,
only to realize there is one word for it all:

Hungry

Panic Attack

It was around 8 p.m. that the wall broke
and the air in my room began rushing out
as though I were in an airplane flying
as fast as my heart beat,
not lying in bed reading
like it was any other Thursday.

If I were in such a place,
I'd politely ask, through gasping breaths,
for a tiny glass of water
and peanuts to grind my teeth on
rather than the neck of the man inside me.
Despite my irrational rage,
I meant no ill will toward him
nor the imaginary stewardess
who not-so-politely denied my requests
and told me, as we began a rapid descent,
to use my remaining time to,
albeit quickly,
go fuck myself.

Instead, I closed my eyes,
clenched my pillow,
a parachute I had no idea how to use,
wished my phone had signal
so that I could leave a voicemail
for a woman I knew wouldn't answer,
and waited for the inevitable end of the ride.

That came many hours later,
around 8:45.
I slept horribly that night,
dreaming of my mouth sewn shut with blood,
a caked crimson mask,
and I with no nails to claw it off,
nor water to wash away this cage
save for the obvious solution to
simply wake up.

Killing Time

Most of the time,
I think there is more to life than voluptuous breasts,

But sometimes,
I look down at my phone and think,

"Hmm, maybe not."

Advice

As a certain saying goes,
"Those who can't do
shouldn't judge books by their covers."

That's the second best advice I've heard,
the first being something my old mentor
once told me after a long shift at the marketplace.

"Write drunk, edit sober,"
He said unto me that day.

Years later, I met a girl named Sammy
in an empty Irish bar, midday.
She showed me a funny comic about eating ass,
and I thought,

"Damn, she looks familiar."

She wasn't, I wasn't,
and we never saw each other again.

If only I could take my own advice.

Profile

You look cute, babe.
It's too bad that your personality is bad,
desperate and kind of pathetic.
A pretty face can't cover that,
not the way you are:
needy, awkward, and,
how do you say?

Not worth it.

But hey, I have a minute to waste,
So tell me:
What's it like to be like you?

Lonely?
Yeah, I figured as much.

And passionate?
Surprising, but interesting.

Fulfilling?
Now that sure is crazy.
Tell me more.

No?
Understandable.

Swipe left

Don't Think

One might think that I'd grow tired
of writing the same thoughts many times over,
yet they are all that I have, still,
on nights and days and nights like this.

One might think that after being told moments ago,
I would know if this one's name ended in an "e" or an "a,"
yet that is as irrelevant to me, and to her as well,
as any of the notions drowning in my mind.

One might think that her braids, vexingly woven,
are more complicated than my pain,
which would be correct, despite
the many flavors rejection comes in.

One might think I'd drive home scowling,
struggling, instead of numb,
yet the path is so familiar,
each street sign becomes the same.

One might think that I'd be beyond fantasies,
like my finding a better story,
yet here I am, preparing another glass
and anticipating writing the same next week.

The Mark of a Writer

The curse of a writer
lies not in which words
he can pluck from his brain,
or she can dream from obscurity,
but from what plagues a mind
too erratic to stand for such reason.

What terrifies most
is what we are burdened with,
must transcribe for posterity.
A horrifyingly holistic trance
is the dance of a pen on paper,
like a demonic knife drawing lines
on skin once thought to be innocent.

If we refuse to sacrifice our
souls already tortured by this world,
one that forsakes us, and us to it,
we are met with a painful gridlock
of inescapable and ravenous emotions
demanding to be loosed from asylum,
bedamning a Fate that locked them
in a body so weak and ill-willed.

To those courageous enough
that they can embrace the madness,
and grow strong from its whims,
blessings are upon them and their work,

either raining from joys above,
erupted from perditions below,
or shades in between, they cannot fathom
yet will demonstrate nonetheless,
for the awakening of wisdom
or a curse of catharsis,
they will write, they will bleed,
they will drown the world in ink.

Libido

When I gazed into the abyss,
it looked directly into my eyes
and begged me to fuck it harder,
which was expected really.

There are many times across days, nights
when the void presses deeper, harder
into my mind to entice me and use
that which I hold dear,
fantasies in the form of memories,
to fulfill its own desires.

It is a tactic that is often
difficult for me to swallow;

I feel the darkness exude over
a soul that craves peace
instead of a desolate encounter yet
finds neither.

It is the vehement hungering
of an illusion that is always
more beautiful than reality,
yet purer than the truth,
that ultimately accumulates in
a single, monstrous emotion:

Loneliness   and   Lust.

Sadness helps me sleep

but not as much as sin does.

When I feel panic leave my body,
when I'm cradled by my misery,
when I believe I am as lonely as
the evening's final star,
there is not a single word
that comes to me,
      except maybe "I miss you,"
that would be as comforting as
even a brush against
a hand so fair
I can believe
it reaches down from nowhere,
across the emptiness between us
to fill it instead inside me
and paint me dreamless rest.

Fevered Scribblings

Dreams never die, only wither.
Dreams never die, but nightmares are forever.
Dreams never die, and neither will we.

   Yet, every body perishes.
   Yet, every soul is sold.
   Yet, every friend betrays.

We are all of these,
   And nothing more.

Sometimes a Sandwich is Just Bread, Meat, and Cheese

Hello, yes, that's me,
beloved Poet,
eccentric, engaging,
and
whatever.

Inspiration,
perspiration,
and all of that bullshit

is what I put up with
        while I
Spin riveting stories,
Craft beautiful verses,
Present bold proclamations
on this elegant stage of mine.

Thank you for asking
if I wanted this wretched "gift" of words
and ability, no compulsion,
to create them from any random thing I find.
        Maybe I just wanted to
Walk in peace,
Lounge around,
Eat my lunch,
Fuck my girlfriend
        (or whatever you "normal" people do).

But no, always about
the grand meaning,
the mystical signs,
the dire unknowns,
the profound ideals,
the things that make you shiver and wonder,
the things that drill me deeper and madder!

    Well screw you,
sometimes a sandwich is

Oh, just reread the title
and leave me the hell alone.

Swine Can at Least Be Eaten

I'm sorry, the humans are trying to talk.
Could you put your babble together elsewhere?

What's that now? You're her mother?
You probably think you know what that means,
but that can't be true,
that would require a level of empathy
greater than that of a bacteria's,
which you have neither the cognition nor dignity of.
Please *do not* demand respect from me
when *you* don't have the capacity to show it to anyone.

You're still here? Oh,

> I shouldn't have to expend my breath on you,
> as I can't fathom why the world wastes any resources
> on what I wouldn't objectively dignify as a "thing,"
> but since you won't be silent and let us live
> without the dead weight of your fat, cancerous form,
> *we* will leave you here, as all will,
> including the worms that will vomit your remains,
> just as sickened as I am by your ever existing!

Good?
> Bye.

Reinstitution

The Crow is flying overhead
planning his next attack,
to leave them all soon left for dead
and bring the glory back.
Grace is falling from the sky
like an angel upon the earth;
with all the power to identify
he must catch her for rebirth

Let's fire on the Pyramid
and set the past ablaze;
the spire on the desert grid
casts shadows on her maze.
Allow the gold ruins to smolder,
for then the future may yet come alive;
dismantle each piece young and older
because illusions cannot survive.

The Crow flies on, with grace in stars
against an ancient, bloodied sky,
to claim victory against kings and scars,
his sole wish is to lift her high.
To eliminate all sorrow
and bring order to the night,
an embrace leads towards tomorrow,
backed by wings of all his might.

I swear we'll burn down the Pyramid

once given that noble chance:
Shedding light to the darkness in which she hid
breaking through the sands of that trance.
From its inferno, a hero I'll rise
and joy will reign throughout her land;
Grace is the phoenix, a dance to the skies,
to walk on each hand in hand.

Cowardice

I'll try my best,
but I can't promise I'll be better

I can only promise I'll be yours,
that I am yours,
and I'll try my best
for that to be enough

Apotheosis

You don't need to sign a contract,
> *Name in your own blood,*

to hear wisdom from above you,
to feel maddened from below you,
to draw power from beyond you.

I drew upon those I connected with,
> *Four lessons did I learn,*

and I used my tribulations
to forge me on life's journey.

From the first experience,
> *Light upon my youth,*

I learned what it meant to love,
to burn with passion and to be chained by it.

From the second, much later,
> *Chaos in a new world,*

I learned what it meant to lie,
to be used and to do so to survive.

From the third, pivotally,
> *Darkest and most beautiful,*

I learned what it meant to fear,
to be strengthened by souls' suffering.

From the fourth and final,
                    Seas separated by now,
I learned what it meant to fail,
to have paradise stolen away by pride.

Each of these burning stars,
                    Every lost laugh and scream,
does blaze and echo inside,
will until memories die with me.

I have embraced their ideals,
                    Emotions and thoughts overwhelming,
to fulfill who I truly am,
to build a safe, secluded future,
to dream until the end.

Logophobia

You've come to this room again,
to empower and to mock me,
with your shadows and wisdom,
in interlocking shades of blackness.

I normally would dance on letters,
let each syllable drip from me,
pen in hand, over ivory pages,
releasing the depth of mind and soul.

Tonight, I do not wish to embrace you,
nor bask in your ordered madness.
For each line taxes heavily
and each word conveys a consequence.
How can I write down the magic,
when all stings like a razor?
How can I justify the venom,
when it will seep beyond these walls?

Yet you are persuasive, persistent,
driving beauty stronger than my heart:
Inspiration, to you, victory,
World and my Love, remorse.

Hotel in Sunrise, Florida

The memory that I have
of you holding my head
gently against your jasmine-scented breast
and, with eyes softly distant as a summer stout,
telling me that I have to let you go

isn't real,
although I wish it was
because then, at least briefly,
I would have been close to your heart.

Instead, I jolt awake to humid air,
bound by a bed overseen by
generic beach paintings and worn wallpaper,
the grating of braggart seagulls in the parking lot
ushering away that foolhardy dream,
and I long to caress the wisps of raven hair
that were only *your* wings to escape with.

The Empty and the Dead

Another glass,
Another game,
More one-off conversations;

My memories,
My dreams,
More desperate poems.

these have nothing in common at all.

Beauty Routine

Every morning, I start my body's machine;
it often stalls, so the best thing to do
is let it lie for a while, hit it a few times,
or pour in water.

I drag it to the bathroom,
sometimes muddling through painful vision
when the light reflects strongly off the porcelain tub.
I stare tiredly, then hatefully, then tiredly again
at the bearded face before me, then sigh.

The routine is the same after that:
I brush my teeth with depression,
Comb my hair with apathy,
Put on a dark green uniform,
Decide against sustenance,
Sigh once again.

I wave my brother goodbye,
wish him well,
and wish for myself
that maybe today,
just for today,
I can be beautiful.

II

Epiphany

The Master's Plan

I once called myself a schemer,
a developer of plans ignoble,
impossible,
and indulgent in nature.
Friends, family?
At best, they were like idols,
unfairly unworthy and
at best they were useful
for my fruitless machinations,
futile attempts at feeling important,
but sooner rather than later,
my pride fell too far
and it wasn't I that brought order to my soul.

I once called myself a dreamer,
maybe I still am,
in the wistful moments before sleep:
I needed them there, needed "her" there,
would have given anything for embrace.
But outside those lonely hours,
I was unmade, my pride shattered
alongside my corruption,
instantaneous, miraculous peace
and in that transformative instant,
it wasn't I that allowed me to be reborn.

I once called myself strong,
and clever,
and beautiful,

the best of all the things
I always wanted to be.
But what am I now? Am I these things and more?
I am the only thing that matters:
I am a son of God.

I'm stronger than I think I am,
but not nearly as strong as I want to be.
Thankfully I don't have to be,
as I reflect His wisdom and grace.
The master plan was never mine,
someday that'll be okay;
my strength is found in Heaven-side,
to grow in that light, I'll stay.

You too are stronger than you think you are,
but maybe not where you want to be,
realize that you don't have to be
to reflect His wisdom and grace.
I don't know the master plan,
and somehow, that's okay,
our strength is found in Heaven-side,
to grow in that light, please stay.

Scents of the Divine

If a soul,
          a pure soul,
has a scent to it,
I would wager it is of
the smoldering incense that
gently floats down from the oaken altar before me.

I base this off of nothing more
than the euphoric peace I feel in this space
and how this potent perfume
melds and resonates with
my own sufficient spirit,
as if its own flickering fire
was keeping the smoke around me
alive.

Cherry Rose Sencha

It's comforting to sit at a bar
with colorful flavors such as
"Energy,"
"Immune System Boost,"
"Stamina,"
and "Calming,"

instead of the fermented
"Self-destruction,"
"Desperation,"
"Incoherence,"
and "Generalized Hatred"
that were prevalent in my old life.

When before I would slide frantically across my phone,
now I gaze around the mahogany tables
and think,
"Laura would love this place,"
and in that moment, unlike so many before,

I smile.

The World Inside Your Eyes

The turbulence of these oceans,
all joy and sorrow in disguise;
I wish for *this* world to be
the world I see in your eyes.

Illusory as much elusive,
reality can not itself bend,
here, time and nature not existing,
all fractures set to mend.

Pure as in the Beginning,
innocence as a child abound,
one place welled up in only,
cascading without a sound.

The tranquil, shimmering ocean
washes away all seeing lies;
please let me stay and rest here,
in the world inside your eyes.

Arrival, 8:40 a.m.

I have only three goals for this trip:

I want to see the mountains,
feel my soul grow as tall as they are
by the wisdom whispering in their shadows,

I want to find her the perfect souvenir,
something as unique as her heart,
as pristine as her presence,

and I want to gather the courage to give it to her smiling,
        saying, "I missed you a lot"
if nothing else but to see a smile in return
and know my return is a welcome one.

So, dear Uncle, shall we begin?

Wish She Were Here

The way that the sun sets over the mountains,
with the light slipping slowly down,
casting a cascade of purples, reds, and pinks,
and juxtaposed against vibrant autumn trees,
dancing amongst falling leaves of indescribable hues,

is the second most beautiful thing I've ever seen.

The first should be fairly obvious.

Still Field Under Scarlet Sky

Surely there must be a word
for missing someone deeply,
yet knowing you'll see them again,
even the day, the time.

      Anticipation? Impatience, perhaps?

This day, this time,
I am at relative peace,
a peace brought on by grace.

Yet in my heart, anxiety looms,
not that of skeptical hope,
not that of fear,
but that of the sheer longing
to weave our souls together again,
linked bodies, minds, and hearts.

      Yes, impatience I believe it is.

Dream Feather

A crimson feather falls...

Fire is like ice, a freezing blaze,
when its heart bears no passion,
no epiphany can abide there
as the flames are choked away.
But ice can be like fire
if all is burned, blown askew,
and crystalized to rebuild the future;
this is a marvelous cycle indeed.

  ...and the dance goes on, descending...

Many can be those who posture
upon the lofty throne of one's life;
the essence of such adoration is determined
by the face of one's chosen heroine:
a demon spills forth poison,
while a queen of light nourishes
and we, the wretch or angel,
may choose to drink from either.

   ...then an updraft comes, redeeming...

Time is cruel and relentless,
like an inconspicuous stream
eroding a mountain slowly;
none escape its maddened flow.
Yet there is hope from its spell,

for though they may breathe and die,
champions, poets, merchants, and all
live, as friends may eventually eternally.

       ...past the clouds within the sky...

There are infinite roads to travel,
colors that can define our space;
there's an equal multitude of guides
that lead us on this defining journey:
strong are the malicious voices
of anger, vanity, fear, and lust,
but the softened roar of love
can still overcome the din.

       ...'til it begins to rest at last...

Wisdom is too amorphous,
and the line is often shrouded
between reality and truth
and all the lies left in between.
As we slumber and walk awake,
these visions ever persist:
to discern the heart of innocence
in everything is the key.

      ...as the feather finally settles,
on still waters of a dream.

Sleep well

little lost boy:

Rest as much as you need,
Dream as much as you can,
Hope as long as you're able.

I will be with you.

A Midnight Promise

No matter how much my mind breaks or my heart hurts,
I will keep my flame alive.

Whether it emblazes the world
or is reduced to smolders,
I will give everything to find out.

No darkness will snuff me,
nor time blow away,
the song in my soul.

Monday Lunchtime

There comes a day in every young man's life
when he impulsively purchases
a container of mac and beer cheese
at the local marketplace
and, permission be damned,
reaches into the pantry for his roommate's bread crumbs,
savory, illegitimate bread crumbs,
to sprinkle across the destined dish,
not for honor,
but for flavor
and for the strength to carry on
with the day, the week, for all eternity.

I am that man
and today
is that day.

An August Afternoon

This is a poem about nothing special:

It's about a single leaf,
torn from its tree by the wind
greeny, veiny, and destined to brown.

It's about a blue countertop,
wet with soap, water, and dedication,
that contrasts aesthetically well
with the travertine paved floor.

It's about an open cardboard box,
folded and taped, but empty,
with no markings to identify its origin.

It's about those old, plastic pads in urinals
that no one knows the proper name of.

It's about an orange,
sliced perfectly and ripe,
spreading sweet citrus scents.

It's about liquid glue.

It's about a red flag at a beach,
literal, not metaphorical.

It's about a freshly dried load of laundry,

warm and clean,
the fresh scent of lavender
masking the inconvenience of the tangled dryer sheet.

It's about the pen that's been clicked uncountable times
and then tossed aside when it became useless
or kept for strangely sentimental reasons.

It's about a bottle of hot sauce
whose drop could burn a tongue for hours,
or whose whole contents couldn't satisfy.

It's about a small bottle of makeup,
maybe worn by an office worker,
maybe by a whore,
but that never judged in either case.

It's about a credit card,
worn, sticky, and frayed,
yet always faithful.

It's about a stationary chair
with violet armrests, sturdy back,
and just the right amount of cushioning.

It's about a backyard pool
with the perfect low level to it
to remind its owners of their childrens' splashes
that made it so.

This is a poem about nothing important:
It's simply about life.

Eye of the Holder

A strand of hair caught in the dryer,
A dirty glass on the countertop,
A leaf on the carpet,
A pencil,

All items that are worthless to some,
      maybe even to you,
but to me, point to profound beauty,
one in my heart, my home,

And is everything I hold dear.

Blue Ballpoint Pen

Have you ever stared at an area of dust in your room?
You know the one:
the spot, or maybe streak,
of gray, thinly fuzzy, hair-infused dirt
in the corner of your lamp or desk or shelf;

have you ever chosen to stare just past it
because your brain was too active to sleep,
but too tired to do anything else?

I have,

except, then, it was more so my heart locking up,
not in an anxiety-ridden, fearful way,
but because it craved to create, to write,
to sing, to conjure great words,
great deeds, great gestures, great needs
to express the beauty and its admiration
of a woman too far now to hold
and too close to envision anything else
besides mad, joyful words, like "love" and "miss,"
and the single thought that maybe,
not tonight, but maybe,   maybe tomorrow,

I should wipe that bit of dust away.

Right Focus

I've found that it's in the moments
that I reflect the hardest
the days drag on,
          drag on,
             drag on,
                that I feel ancient, lack fire-breathing,
                  am at a loss of words
          for the newest way to describe her beauty,
      her kindness,
     her humor,
  her skill,
but it's also then that I remember
not to fixate on grandiosity,
simply enjoy the journey
and the everyday joy
of all of the above.

Just an Observation

An old sketchbook full of insults
creates the backdrop in her mind,
each character whispering within,
each slur an embarrassed pencil-stroke.

See, the girl that holds it doesn't understand;
uses such words as "dumb" and "useless,"
disgusting lies that one could ever make up,
if the untruth is the truest ugly.

Just an observation, but the somehow invisible
kaleidoscope of beauty and virtue
are obvious to me and all our friends,
and we wish she'd see too.

You know a thing about losing sleep?
I know it's the same for her sleeping
on each light within, favoring instead
unfair contrasts, ignoring her heat.

For what it's worth, you're
the funniest I know,
certainly kind,
powerfully skilled,
and highly charming,
so try not to be so

hard on the girl that doesn't understand,

using such words like "stupid" over and over,
inappropriate lies against someone so great;
we defy such self-deprecation.
I've seen it going 'round, I won't be silent anymore
about the art before you and all you are,
beautifully clear to me who sees it well.

Joke about it again and I'll scream it to hell!

The World Through Stained Glasses

When I look around me,
at swaying palm trees,
        green fingers waving to all passing by,
at magnificent skyscrapers,
        windows winking as they light up each evening,
at flowers and fields and roads,
        each with a story, each alive and moving,
at the smiling faces of those I meet,
at the friendly faces of those I know,
at the radiant face of one I love,

I see a wondrous world, yes;
I see more:
I see joy, hurt, acceptance, wonder, frustration, sadness,
wistfulness, happiness, and compassion.
I see heart.

I know she sees these too,
I can see them reflected in her shining, oaken eyes.
I see soul.

Yet where I see completion in the fingerprint of the Creator
        weaving through all things,
I see eyes that long to see more, but refuse,
        vehemently deny such notions because it is too bright,
so remain not in darkness, but incompletion.

She believes I see illusion,
can see it reflected in my sanguine, oaken eyes.
She sees soul.

We see none,
We see all,

But how I wish to see a world where eyes see truly,
eyes that witness beauty in all its shades,
        present, whole, and holy,
eyes that lock with each other, blend together,
        crying tears of rejoicing in each other and our God.

Icons and Idols

The hardest lesson I had to learn,
when it came to faith and the Universe,
was that God is separate from His people,

to learn that
Jesus is more than my pastor,
Mary is more than my mother,
that He above is greater than they on Earth
and they are who they choose to be:
Icons or idols.

Icons lead others to truth,
they are beautiful and direct to beauty,
just good enough to point up to goodness.
They belong in churches, raised up,
in alleyways, stooping down to the needy,
on the brightest hills because
they've been to the darkest valleys
and have been reborn by grace and humility.

Idols are lies incarnated,
appear beautiful, but are hollow as gilded coffins,
self-indulgent, arrogant, lead only to ruin.
They usurp the place of God on Earth,
enforce service to others to serve only themselves,
place themselves at the pulpit
hoping you never look up from it
and realize there is anything more.

Icons aren't perfect, but they strive for worthy grace;
Idols believe they are perfect, but will never be worthy.

Icons know they aren't God and let God fill in their gaps;
Idols pretend to be God and make up gods to fill the gaps.

Icons are treasures,
the ultimate gold that builds up a soul,
helps it know everything it was meant to be;
Idols are traps,
will offer false sustenance until the moment the bar snaps,
then choke as souls breathe no more.

Icons are people to cherish and walk with,
will expand the love you give
so you can grow in Love together;
Idols cannot love and always walk alone.

The next time you meet someone to believe in,
a stranger or a friend,
ask yourself if they're an icon or an idol,
if they point upward to Heaven
or only at themselves
and remind yourself
that icons are flowers meant to flourish in your heart,
while idols are cancers and will be cleansed,
as a certain prophet once said,
and pray what to do with such a person,
embrace, redeem, or expel,
what the best way is,

then ask yourself too,
"Am I an icon or an idol;
Do I elevate myself or humbly reveal more,
Am I full of lies or do I channel the truth?"
because, in that moment,
the truth may just surprise you.

Discernment

I know that I could,
but should
I
rally the phantoms of the past and present,
the selfish and the beautiful,
wicked and wise,
venomous and true,
the broken and the redeemed?

If we march together at Heaven's discretion,
It's signal,
Grace,
then let it be for the future,
not for friends, nor fame,
but always for soul,
Us.

I know that I could,
but should

Reintroduction

I used to believe in flying on;
alone I planned each attack.
I was strengthened in my crying on,
and in glory I'd never look back.
Then I felt a grace so strong
through an angel upon the earth;
a power that could be no wrong,
so I received a greater rebirth.

Now I live for Him and her
that have shown me a greater path.
I feel His joy, I feel her pain,
soon all shall feel our wrath.
She doesn't need my saving,
yet I'll champion just the same;
brothers, sisters, please join me
in ending cruel darkness's game.

Let's burn down the Golden Land,
set fire to all their lies;
The filth that swarms her graceful hand
will be left as food for flies.
Allow dawn to cover the flooring,
as true art envelopes the walls,
our destiny never left boring,
and Light filling all of our halls.

We fly on together, celestial wings,

blue soaking the once scarlet sky.
Stars have fallen as have their rings
and though I used to wonder why,
I know now that He has chosen her
and I, in likewise kind
to transcend this life into further
until Heaven we both shall find.

Together we'll burn down the Golden Land
and forge a world all of our own.
Upon its pyre we shall both stand
and in holiness forever be grown.
A hero I'm not, but a servant I'll rise,
Prayers offer to King and for Queen:
grace *is* the phoenix, a dance to the skies,
a beauty now never unseen.

Smile

I would burn the whole world to the ground
if it would put a smile on my beloved's face,
but it's precisely that she would never want me to
that grants her that status in my heart

And I would hug Hell happily
if it meant she'd never know pain again,
despite knowing she would never wish such sacrifice;

I suppose only one of us would get what we want.

Still, I hope for a world where neither of us suffer,
where I get over my stubborn will to be a hero
and simply enjoy the glow of that smile.

After all,
she's usually right about this kind of thing.

Manifest

I had a dream last night,
the same one I have every day,
where only the two of us
Smile as we sip our coffee,
Laugh over lunchtime,
Break for our own time,
Dance after dinner,
Snuggle until we sleep.

Then, I have that dream again,
of when only I dreamed of this life,
until it became our beautiful reality
and neither of us could imagine a better one.

Shower

I often feel your visions press into me.

Sometimes I call upon them,
when I feel deviously, manipulatively nostalgic.

Usually, they arrive unannounced,
always playing out the same:
You insist how "wrong it is not to marry you"
and I, in turn, remind you that
"it was supposed to be us against the world,
instead you made it the world against me."

Then, rarely, yet more frequently every night,
in the void between dream and reality,
I'm held in the arms of our Creator,
feel His torrential breath and giant heartbeat,
and know that "hope is all that I have,
but hope is all that I need."

Dawn

I had never expected the last star burning to be yours,
the weakest of all, yet ever the most persistent,
cruel in its glowing, casting pain from what should have been
peace.

For when you say "I miss you," I add, "but not *that* much,"
and when you say "I love you," I add, "but not more than
them."

I had always thought that I couldn't abide by the light,
not expecting that you would shut me away from it,
never escaping that bushel basket except in times of
convenience.

For when you said "I wish you were here," I added, "and as I
would have you be,"
and when you said, "You're my best friend," I added, "only
because I have no others."

I had strived for our world, thinking she wanted the same;
now I realize that hers was all that ever mattered.
Thus, the last star finally fades from the sky
as it flickers far beyond from where I once gazed longingly up,
leaving me to bask freely in the serenity of the rising sun.

Stardust

It   was
    just   a
                Dream,
the   only
          thing
                            real
    about   it

    was that awkward smile that she does

   and   that's
      what   kept
    it
                            from
      being   a

        Nightmare.

Waiting for a Table

What are you trying to tell me,
little brown bird chirping,
frolicking in the sand,
splashing it across your beak and body
like a gray, earthen fountain?

Is it your thesis on innocence,
a reminder to appreciate the small things?
Is it your outlook on creation,
to savor the land we've been given?
Are you asking for help or attention,
from within a tiny, sandy plight?
Or are you expressing a simple joy,
while the grains graze your feathers
and you gaze around in surprise and wonder?

I can't understand your words,
but I envy your enthusiasm,
laugh along inside,
wish I could join in your revelry
and fly away just as carefree.

Sobering Up

I didn't belong in California
despite the sparks that glistened
in my chest every time that I heard
the melodies that rose from the Boardwalk,
or the way that I stared out
perhaps too longingly from my perch
at the possibility-filled Pacific.

I may say that I always tried
but couldn't muster the right spirit,
the strength it took to "make it"
in a land that is determined
to strip aside all inhibitions
and carry me towards my dreams
on the wings of blind ambitions.

I never belonged in California,
couldn't hold the beauty in my veins
or an engine that could compete;
ignoring the encouragement
of agents, aspirants, and controllers,
coming down from the drowning din,

I see
it wasn't I that was truly wrong.

A Certain Auto Dealership

Do not discount immediately
the beauty in a corporate hall:
the shining, freshly polished floors
that reflect flourishing fluorescent,
the energizing aroma of coffee brewed
when its refreshing bitterness is needed,
the harmonic tapping of acrylic nails on keys,
of pages flipping, fingers swiping in
the blissfully spacious waiting room.

Take care to observe the suits’
meticulously pressed regalia,
glistening white teeth,
rhythmically squeaking leather on the
aforementioned flawless floor,
as they pass towering sculptures
of silvery silicon and hidden
gold.

Sure, the lying lights and
manipulative smiles may stand
hollow in a place that’s
simply too normal,

but if we can’t find beauty everywhere,
is there even beauty to be found
at all?

Surprise Party

One man looks shocked, but only by a little.
A woman smiles wistfully for reasons I couldn't guess at.
Another man stares past the wooden boxes, as if
contemplating his storied life,
while yet another enjoys munching on the sandwiches
provided, intentionally ignoring.
But most listen intently to the speaker at the front of the
room.

I myself speculate whimsically about my future
alongside amusing myself by the wonderful people-watching
you can find
being the youngest person in a room full of the elderly
listening to how to plan a funeral.

Always, Always

Hot cheese,
Warm bread,
Savory brews,
and the company of compatriots
all make life worth living,

at least while she's not around;
Then, life is so worth so much more.

Simplicity in the Meaning of Life's Deepest Art

Three
word
poem.

Four?

A Toast to F#

Tonight I raise my glass
to a savior note,
whom without its minor appearance,
another day would have been wasted
solely on whining and wishing to not toast alone.

Instead, I've remembered that even an eighth note of progress
is progress worth noting and living for,

and I'll certainly drink to that.

A Bottle of Dr Pepper

I was almost killed one night
by what my ex-girlfriend described as
"a miserable loser with no future,"
but was really just a defeated man.

On the night I almost took my life
by driving off a bridge at full speed,
there was only one thing that I wanted,
save for my own demise:

A bottle of Dr Pepper.

So it was that I,
with perceived hours left to live,
walked into the nearest supermarket
and purchased the fizzy beverage,
enjoying one last earthly comfort
as I walked out the automatic doors.

My plan would have easily transpired,
if not for a voice calling to me
as I walked across the parking lot,

      "Hey man, how's it going?"

I turned to see a young man,
only a few years older than myself,
eyes sparkling with something I lacked,

a smile sweeter than the drink in my hand,
wave to me from an open SUV's trunk
and I prepared myself to give my remaining cash
to another begging bum.

At no time did the man ask for spare change, however,
and when I gruffly told him that I wasn't well,
that *of course* it was about lost love,
he smiled widely, empathetically,
and told me he understood hardship.

See, he and his beloved,
a woman I now noticed also sitting
in the expanded trunk as I walked over to the vehicle,
were on their own, barely surviving,
with said vehicle as their home.

He asked my name and gave me his
and, with another radiant smile,
relayed to me that he was as joyful as can be.
After all, he had Love,
something he valued above all else,
And he had Hope,
in the form of the factory job he had started earlier.

Tommy told me that he was truly blessed,
and with a gentle hand on my shoulder,
reminded me that I was too,
that I would find my dreams someday,
that my journey would be fulfilled,
that I'll "get there."

I was awestruck, empowered,
if only enough, just enough even,
but somehow more than enough.

Fighting tears, I thanked him for his kindness when I needed
it most,
and offered him free food,
should he ever find himself at the restaurant I worked at,
before we said our goodbyes.

He never did come in for that meal,
and she never said a word,
but I *know* that on that night,
a night shrouded in shadow and circumstance,
God sent two angels to a dim parking lot
to save an inspired man, who drove home safely,
to live and to hope another day.

Friend

"Don't call me that,"
She cried from across the pavement
while the dense spring air
hung over both of our hearts,
like the deepest delusion of one
who never wishes to return to war
yet doesn't realize the battle still smolders.

"But that is what you wanted,
isn't it,"
I wistfully replied
in my mind only since
all that escaped my mouth
was an apology accompanied by
what even I thought was a genuine smile.

The night, the week, the month
passed without any other such incident:

No furtive glances while the other wasn't looking,
No arm-locking that wasn't actually awkward,
as we each convinced ourselves of in the moment,
No stranger remarks for us to dismiss as jest;

Just praise for who we knew each other to be,
Encouragement in our aspirations and careers,
Loud laughing at jokes that certainly
wouldn't have been as funny delivered by someone else,
Just drinks and walks and meals and secrets

shared because trust was consistently abundant.

No expectations or lost resolutions,
Just time and all the joy it entails;

And by the end of our story,
that will always be enough for me.

Hi Tired

I'm a boy who knows what it's like
to lose sleep,
to feel incomplete,
to let that emptiness keep you from peace.

Hi All the Time,
I'm one who believes you deserve better,
who knows you shouldn't have to trundle
through shadows that sow misery,
unjustly, unfairly,
infinitely undeservedly.

Hi Always,
I'm the boy that wants to change your life
but has no idea how,
who stupidly but bravely
would fight to find your happiness,
awake, asleep, every moment in between,
far away or at your side.

Hi,

I'm just a man,
unfocused on the outside too,
yet with a will ever-vibrant,
ever longing for a better life
for you, for us, for whatever it takes
to give you strength and the laughter I hold,
with a smile, a listen, or an eternal embrace.

Philosophize

Insert grandiose construct here

Describe to me how it stampedes through the icy cosmos
How it burns your soul like ethereal embers
How it manipulates Life like a demented puppet master

Tell me how Time or Space or Fate
Has tormented your ironclad mind
Or resonated with your inner echoing voice
In arrogant agreement or staunch opposition

Demonstrate the Darkness and the Light
That decimate society and
Drain the human condition,
The Worlds that feed the void between your words
Or whatever you claim everything to be.

I'll humbly show you my love,
and there will be no question which is greater.

Lady Best

Behold the woman, of all ladies best:
Chestnut eyes of the deepest strain,
alluring joy and the slightest pain,
undeserved for one so blessed,
short-waved hair like an ocean's crest,
drapings that others may falsely find plain,
though not for I, will not stop my refrain
in praise of the beauty of this Lady Best.

Abounding light shines from her face,
round and radiant like the sun before,
an equally ivory smile pristine
lavishes laughter across all this space.
I sing joyfully, proud into forevermore
of her dazzling wonder and beauty serene.

Hierophant Moon

It is the role, the purpose,
of the Moon
to reflect the light of the Sun,
to be inferior to it,
thus existing, created for,
the darkness of the night.

To acknowledge this,
for the Moon itself to understand this,
is not self-deprecation,
but is to be natural, to be ordered.
To deny this truth
is to deny its place, its glory,
its own irreplaceable gift,
and to pretend otherwise
is prideful folly.

The Moon delights,
as I do,
in the shadows, in unorthodox beauty,
and we find our comfort
as a brightness in the night and
among the company of the Stars.

Where the Violets Grew

Long have I prepared for a worthy crown,
never thinking that it'd sit upon your head
      (that's a lie, I knew soon after we met).

Great have I thirsted for inspiration,
not realizing the greatest was from you
      (gifted thoroughly from Heaven).

Strangely have I suffered, joyfully,
from the laughter of the peace we share
      (so close, so far, so intimate, so alone).

Bright does my heart burn alive
since it found belonging next to yours
      (there's no one I'd trust more).

And though it isn't the home I once dreamed of,
I wouldn't trade this for all of the world
      (or for even a second without you around).

Dial Tone

My dear Aunt once told me,
the test of loving someone
is that when something good happens in your life,
they're the first person you want to tell.

It's not the fluttery feeling in your heart,
or the peace when they're around,
or the void when they are not,
the frantic crying for an entire day
when you're not sure when you'll see them again,
even if its been hours since the last,
still you lash out at yourself and

No, the trademark, so I'm told,
is the desire to share all news with them,
to ask about their day or week
and genuinely care about their answer.

It's not the longing for a life united,
or relaying stories from a joyous past,
or attending gatherings of family and friends
and turning to laugh with the person that's not there,
or flipping through old photos and point, shouting,
"see, that was me, wasn't I adorable,"
and then reminiscing some more and be embarrassed
but not wanting to stop, never wanting to stop,
instead wanting to hear *their* stories too and
look at *their* old photos

and maybe argue, maybe cry together,
but it wouldn't matter because at the end of the night
we'd both still have each other
and at the end of the night,
that would always
be   enough.

My Aunt imparted that wisdom to me;
I'm not sure if it's true or not,
but in that moment, when it happened,
all I wanted was to tell you.

In the Oven

This is my burden;
I carry it joyfully, but
I don't carry it for you or anyone else.

This is my life,
elated by the grace I've been given,
seared by the path that I've chosen
and would again without hesitation.

This is my heart,
alive and rippling,
tempered and primed,
wounded and strong,
with a hole built into it,
as it has always been.

It is mine,

but if you want it,
when you can hold it without breaking it,
when you can join with it without breaking,
merely say the word.

In the meantime,
I'll keep it warm for you.

Purpose

I used to write so that others could feel
the same pain that I did.

Now, I write so that others can know
my adoration of Life
(and all her wondrous beauty).

But someday, I believe I'll write so that others can chuckle
when they read a little line
that adds just a bit of humor to their lives and, if I'm lucky,
joy.

III

Into the Future

Fog

There is a turbid purpose
within the fog,
across the world,

the one I know:
incomplete, the present.

Ominous shrouding,
gray mist glissading
as moisture on my skin
serves only to damper
the vision I desire.

I see silhouettes:
outlines of us,
outlines of too many
obscuring forms of
formless faces,
mocking, judging,
heavy as hopeless
to those who cannot
see the sun.

Cast under its cloak,
I walk, then sleep;
my heart is hazy still,
yet with will to carry on

to the one beyond
the fog of the future.

Reflecting droplets,
dim glory permeating
as lovely clouds caress
slick forms, sleepy and safe
in the vision that we've claimed.

Soothed in its embrace,
We laugh, make love;
our hearts concealed together
as a single ray of sunlight
cuts through to us from above.

Future Forward

I hope you have enjoyed,
perhaps been enlightened by,
what our dual heroes have dreamed
and shared with you in this collection.

Poor Desolation,
his own emptiness,
his inward-facing insecurity,
the war he waged against himself,
drove him to seek hollow comfort
in those whom could never sustain,
no matter how desperately he willed it.

He was blind, yes,
but not hopeless,
despite what he believed,
and though his legacy survives,
always tempts in lonely times,
may he overcome, find lasting peace,
and may you, reader, as well.

Wonderful Epiphany,
his renewal,
his outbound empathy,
the mercy he gratefully received,
led him to embrace the beauty
in health, happiness, and trust
in his family and companions
that strengthen him as

conduits of the greatest grace.

He has changed, yes,
but his journey is not over,
nor is perfected from ever onward,
rather he must be devoted, determined,
not out of obligation nor habit,
by belief in the goodness of those united;
may you, reader, find such motivation as well.

As we close the curtain now,
remember well these visions and lessons
and though there may be those that do not understand
        this cautionary darkness,
        this revolutionary light
can and will inspire us
as we strive for an end to
isolation,
self-deprecation,
disorder,
and, most importantly, fear,
in this world and for all time.

Notes/References

Tina Turner is counted among the visionaries in "They'll Drain You Slowly, Man" due to the best-selling hit "What's Love Got to Do with It" from her 1984 album *Private Dancer*. This is not meant for sarcasm; it's an absolute banger.

The last stanza of "Spotlight" references William Shakespeare's famous *As You Like It* quote:
> All the world's a stage,
> And all the men and women merely players

"Snowy Winter Ale" contains references and commentary to "Stopping by Woods on a Snowy Evening" by Robert Frost.

For legal purposes, the popular and delicious potato crisps brand Pringles, by Kellog's, in no way contributes to the speaker dying in "The Food Chain is More of a Cycle."

The opening lines of "Libido" are a modification of Friedrich Nietzhche's infamous *Beyond Good and Evil: Prelude to a Philosophy of the Future* quote:
> And if you gaze for long into an abyss, the abyss gazes also into you.

In "Icons and Idols," the exact quote of what the Biblical prophet once said comes from the book of Ezekiel 36:25 (NABRE):

I will sprinkle clean water over you to make you clean; from all your impurities and from all your idols I will cleanse you.

It should not be taken as fact that a "Bottle of Dr Pepper" or any other carbonated soft drink by Keurig Dr Pepper Inc. could help save a life, but it should not outright be dismissed either.

Although most of the poems in this collection are written in free verse, "Lady Best" is an homage to the fixed form style of the Petrarchan sonnet, perfected by iconic Italian poet Francesco Petrarca.

The title phrase of "Where the Violets Grew" is the direct answer my great-grandfather James, a child of Italian immigrants to America, always gave when his daughter-in-law, my grandmother, would ask where his family's home once was.

Acknowledgements

This book has been a long time in the making and it would be next to impossible to thank everyone who played a role in my journey to its completion. That said, there are a few standout individuals whom without their assistance, guidance, inspiration, and advice, *Desolation and Epiphany* would not exist as it is today.

Firstly, I would like to thank Adina Perullo, my cousin and expert editor, who helped hone this collection and encourage me through it. I deeply wish that she could have been here to see it completed fully, but I like to think she'd be glad to see the readers of this book added to all of the lives she touched.

I would also like to thank the numerous writers and fans of the written word who have advised on my work over the years: Alex, Amorita, Bekah, Brittany, Dom, Frank, Garrett, Jes, Nikki, Sophie Klahr, Uncle Robert, and especially Karla, who has sat with me at many an open mic and supported me throughout my literary adventure.

In a big way, I would like to thank the best artist in the world, possibly in the whole universe, and one of the coolest people I know, Ashton Lay, for providing the incredible cover art for this book. I couldn't have imagined a better illustration for the cover of this collection and I couldn't be more proud of how the final publication turned out due to your talent, hard work, and keen eye for aesthetics.

I feel abundantly blessed to have amazing people in my life who have walked with me and continue to stand by me in love and comradery. Although there's no possible way I could list everyone by name, know that I am grateful every day for my family and friends, for the people who have put up with my bullshit in dark times and celebrated with me in the brightest ones.

To the Lord above, who has unconditionally and miraculously given me the grace to be the person I am today, and to everyone who has been a part of my story thus far and as far as it goes: Thank You!

About the Author

James W. A. was born and raised in the Tampa Bay area in Florida. After graduating from the University of South Florida, St. Petersburg's Honors College, he published his first book, *In the Library*, in 2015. Since then, he has honed his ever-evolving, contemporary style, both creatively and as a professional content writer. While moving away from the dark subjects of younger days, James W. A. seeks to use his experiences, joys, sorrows, and wonders he sees in the world around him to lead others to truth and beauty and share meaningful stories to last the ages.

Thejameswa.com
Instagram: @thejameswa